Copyright 2023 by Matt Tomlinson – All rights reserved.

It is not legal to reproduce, duplicate, or send any part of this document in either electronic means or printed format. Recording of this publication is prohibited.

Chapter	Page

Foreword

For those that do not know, in most books, at the start, there is a thing called Foreword, which is defined as:

"A Foreword is a piece of writing, sometimes placed at the beginning of a book or other piece of literature."

Typically written by someone other than the primary author of the work, it often tells of interaction between the writer of the foreword and the book's primary author or the story the book tells.

The reviews on the next page are about the first book published 'Business Book for 10 Year-Olds...WHY?' they are currently on Amazon in the review section.

A truly illustrative and inspirational book for all our youngsters today… pen at the ready! Matt Tomlinson is a true leader, oozing confidence and passion in all he does for charity and helping people of all age groups! A must-buy! - CARLA AMIS.

An excellent, well-written book. Lots of interactive content to help children stay engaged and practical ways to help them start their own business, things you won't learn in school.

My 8-year-old daughter loves it and is already making plans for her new business.

Would highly recommend it, especially as proceeds go to two children's charities - Cllr EMILY GLEAVES.

Amazing book for kids who want to get a head start in life. I have already passed this on to my three sons to read. DAVID JOHN BARNES.

A great read to get your little ones thinking more about money and how they can start earning and saving! – HALEY SALE.

Fantastic book! I bought two copies of this for my 11-year-old twins. Putting the Xbox pad down and food for thought for them. Well written, a good read (and I am deffo older than 10).10/10 – AMAZON READER.

A good grounding book that all under 12-year-olds should read, so good I bought two. Well done Mr. Tomlinson; look forward to the next one – <u>Mrs. D A GREEN.</u>

As a 40 yr old, I wish I had read this at 10 years old, although I have 6 yr old twins, so I have lots of information to form their thoughts on saving and being business-minded Thank you cannot wait for the next book – <u>VIKKI WOOD.</u>

Unlock your child's financial success: The must-have book for raising money – Smart Kids. YouTube video testimonial <u>KEV G</u>

Amazing book for kids AND adults!!
This book is a must-read for kids and adults. There's so much wisdom to learn from it regarding money, business and life. My 9-year-old son loves it, and it has already inspired him to start his business when he's older. I also loved it; it's written in such an engaging and inspiring way. This book should be taught as part of the school curriculum! <u>CHRIS</u>

Introduction

This book is written in the most simplified way. WHY? Because I don't have the best academic background. I didn't do well in school. I couldn't read or write, and I still can't spell to this day. Thank the computer techies of this world for inventing smartphones and computers and the super team who came up with the idea of SIRI or Google, where you can simply ask:

"How do you spell…..?"

Without this, I would never have got the book started, not to mention finished.

You may or may not know this, but this book is the second part of a 5-part series.

1. BB410YOWHY…

2. BB416YOWHY…

3. BB418YOWHY…

4. BB421YOWHY…

5. AUTOBIOGRAPHY…

I want to write five books to create more awareness about two of the children's charities based in my local area. Incubabies & Claire House Children's Hospice. My daughter was an incubabie; she had severe difficulty breathing as soon as she was born, with various other complications.

After receiving the most invaluable care and attention for eight weeks, she survived and has become one of the kindest-hearted, most caring humans I have encountered.

She loves looking after children in her current role, she also attends college, studying Phycology, I.T. and Law.

At 16 years old, her personal journey has only just begun.

This book is designed to help and guide you to your purpose and role in life and employment or as a business owner. YES, a business owner at 16...!

Chapter 1 – Self Comparison

Don't base your happiness
off of other people's lives.

more successful?   better life?

Stop comparing your life to other's,
and focus on what's best for YOU.

chibird

The school systems have said, since you started school, that if you are an A-grade student, you will be successful; if you do not have any grades, you will not.

They categorise you into groups after you have done your tests to make you feel that is all you're worth. They do this so you will not drag the A-graders down or so you don't feel pressured and always last in the class.

Believe me when I say this: It is the biggest mistake teachers make. I know many people who have zero grades, have become some of the most successful business owners, and earn five times more than a headteacher.

Most of your parents, nans and grandads have told you from a young age, "Oh, I wish you were like... (child's name) so you can be better, or I wish you would behave like. (child's name)."

Because this has been instilled in our brains from an early age, we feel the need to constantly compare ourselves to others.

For many of you reading this now, life can be tough; you will get knocked down, and things will not go your way.

At 16 years of age, you will have more added pressure from your friends, the reason being that some of them will have a part-time job, and they may have been given an opportunity from their work experience placement.

If you haven't got a job already, you will feel bound to find employment so you do not feel like a failure.

Your friends will have more money each month, even talking about driving lessons, etc. You might have applied for twenty or thirty jobs and not had any feedback from them.

You Will Start Doubting Yourself!

Is it me?

I am doing something wrong?

Why haven't I got a job?

Please remember – DO NOT compare your life to anyone else's. There will be dozens of reasons why they will have a job and you don't.

Let's think about why you might not be destined to have a "job".

You are reading Business Book For 16-Year-Olds…WHY? for a reason.

Your destiny is to be a LEADER and not be LED.

You should not settle for just a "job" because you think that you should. You would be naturally guided to THINK OUTSIDE THE BOX of ways to make money.

In the next chapter, we will cover jobs for a 16-year-old and self-employment jobs for a 16-year-old.

See which one you feel drawn to.

Chapter 2 – Jobs for a 16-Year-Old

Write in the boxes what jobs you think you can do at 16 years of age.

Question...?

Can you think of your friends and what jobs they have? Once you have thought of them, write down their job title in the boxes. Fill the boxes up as much as possible.

Employed – Working for Someone Else

Working for someone may include – fast food restaurants such as McDonald's, KFC, Burger King, Dominos, and Subway.

In retail – High Street shops, H&M, Boss, Beaverbrook's, Primark, Rolex, or small local independent shops or outlets within your area. They might even work for a bank, or work in a factory, etc.

Self-Employed – Working for Yourself

Working as a self-employed person - Candle Wax Artist, Face Paint Artist, Social Media Marketing (for other businesses), Dog Walker, House Sitting for owners on holiday, Only Fans, YouTube video creator, Product Selling Advisor, Children's Entertainer, D.J., construction trades, Uber Driver, etc.

Now, colour the boxes in the same colours as the subheadings for Employed and Self-Employed.

At the age of 16, are any of your friends or you in the self-employed category? If the answer is YES, you should be super proud because you've decided on your future and acted. You/they have a vision and a goal.

What job do you currently do or see yourself doing?

Write on the lines…………………………………

Are you fully happy in your job role?

…………………………………………………………

…………………………………………………………

13

Do you feel you have a purpose in life?

....

....

If the answer is NO, why do you think this is?

....

....

If the answer is YES, then well done you.

"Happiness is the new success".

Did you know that data from the Gallup World Poll (a survey of the happiness of adults in 132 countries around the WORLD) show that richer people in any country do not always feel happier than poorer ones? And beyond $75,000 a year in the United States, more money does not buy any more happiness (at all) for the average U.S. citizen earning about this amount.

Being rich might make you think you are happier, but it does not necessarily make you feel any happier.

This is why it is imperative that you should not settle for anything that you feel unhappy about in your job role. You must seek until you find true fulfilment.

The only way to find true fulfilment is to start at the very bottom of any career and work your way to the top. Which, might I add, is never-ending.

I speak with business owners who have been super successful in their careers and who still get up every morning to try and better themselves every day.

The biggest fear for most people when starting a business is FEAR OF FAILURE. I hear things like, what if I fail and my friends or family laugh at me or say I told you so?

Or what if I put my heart, soul, and energy into this, and it fails? I have wasted my time.

It's better to live a life saying, "I am glad I gave that a go," rather than "I wish I did that."

In business, you must FAIL...!!! Remember, this means FIRST ATTEMPT IN LEARNING.

If you are not failing, you are not trying.

You are reading this book for a reason: you want MORE. You want to GIVE IT A GO. Do not procrastinate; you may think, I'm only 16, I've got all the time in the world. Believe me, as you get older, the years go by faster.

If you are reading this book and you are 20, 30, 40, 50, 60, or even seventy years of age, it does not matter; you must remember;

"It's never too late to be great."

"You do not have to be great to start, but you have to start to be great".

"The Journey of 1000 miles starts with a single step."

Continuing to read Business Book For 16-Year-Olds…WHY? You will be guided to the importance of having multiple streams of income.

Chapter 3
Multiple Streams Of Income

In your own words, write in the boxes below what you think this means and how you would do it?

There are nine spaces for you to fill out; if you fill out all nine and need space for more, there are blank pages at the back of the book. I will say that if you fill the full nine and you haven't googled it, you are seriously on your way to becoming successful.

At 16, I was out with my school friends most nights and weekends, up to mischief. Ah, the good old days. Yet you are here, reading this book, thinking of multiple ways to earn money, WELL DONE. 😊

Multiple streams of income are what most people call a "Side Hustle" or another way of earning money in addition to your normal job.

See the list below for seven online side hustles for teens.

1. Get paid to take surveys.
2. Start a blog or podcast.
3. Monetize social media, like a TikTok or YouTube channel.
4. Freelance on Fiverr.
5. Manage social media accounts.
6. Flipping clothing or other items.
7. Watch videos or play games with a site like Swagbucks.

Some of you reading this book might be sitting here thinking,

"I haven't even got a job, never mind a side hustle".

The side hustles mentioned are all online. If you do some serious research into one that feels best suited to you, you can start straightaway; plus, if you market it right (as in promote it well) on social media platforms, people will buy into it, you'll start seeing regular and this could be your full-time job.

I recently had a conversation with an amazing friend called Simon, who sells all his unwanted clothes. He averages about £200.00 per month!!
He sells clothes that are slightly faded, don't fit him, or he's just simply had them for a long time.

As a 16-year-old, I would assume you have a lot of clothes you don't wear anymore due to outgrowing them.

You could sell them to, one, make room in your wardrobe, and, two, make some additional money.
You will start to feel a "buzz" when your clothes start selling.

NO ONE TALKS ABOUT THEIR MONEY; they see it as a dirty word, and some are ashamed of it.

They lead a double life; again, this comes down to self-comparison, "Trying to keep up with the Jones" is a famous saying in America. Once you speak freely about money and tell everyone how grateful you are for it, and you appreciate every single penny, money comes in abundance.

I can guarantee there will not be many authors or business owners telling you about their finances in such detail. What I am showing you is the huge difference between going to work and trading your time for money and money going to work for you whilst you sleep!!

YES, money goes to work whilst YOU sleep...Zzzzzz

1 - Main Source of income – MDfitout Ltd.

Office and shop fitting company. I am a 50/50 shareholder, which means I split everything with my business partner, Dave. This is where I trade my time for money – I go to work, and it pays me back.

2 - Extras in TV shows.

No one knows about this apart from my immediate family, so this can be our little secret; don't tell anyone. SShhhhh.

3 - Government tax payments called working tax credits.

More about government tax payments is in the next chapter and in detail in the Business Book for 18-Year-Olds...WHY?

20

4 – Book Sales.

Proceeds/royalties from the books I write all go to charity, but it's a stream of income you can easily do yourself.

5 – Investments.

Investment in the stock market builds up by an average of 9% to 10% per year.
More on investments and my portfolio in the next chapter.

6 - Networking Events.

I have set up a networking event called 3 C Networking. It pays a little, but a little over time becomes a lot; that's the main information about investing. Compounding over time.

Emily is the co-founder with me; not only do we get a very small percentage of income, but we get more knowledge due to empowered, motivated entrepreneurs who attend the meeting & share their ideas; knowledge is more powerful than anything; it brings confidence, confidence brings a sense of pride.

7 – Investments (crypto)

Since 2017, I have invested in cryptocurrencies, which are very volatile; I am unable to give any data for my investment returns (ROI) due to sporadic impulsive investments and not regular monthly payments as I do with my stocks and shares portfolio.

8 – Personal Pension portfolio.

Through one of my businesses, I have had a payment plan of £300.00 per month directly from the business for a number of years, which is currently compounding and earning interest daily for my retirement. This annual payment of £3,600.00 is offset against our annual corporation tax bill at each year-end of accounts. More about this in Business Book For 18-Year-Olds...WHY?

9 – Savings.

I currently put £400.00 per month into a Lloyds super saver account, which gives me 6% ROI (return of investment per annum/year). Money going to work. I wrote about this in the Business Book For 10-Year-Olds...WHY? which is the book before this one? If you haven't read it, it will be worth reading to provide a gentle reminder of Saving, Investing and Spending the simplified way.

Future Streams Of Income – (Currently Working Towards).

10 – Mattsmotivationuk (on all social media platforms).

On so many occasions, I have been told, "You should be a motivational speaker. People would pay for you to give them a boost of energy, businesses would pay for you to give their team some drive, and people would pay for you to help them become more positive."

At the start of 2023, I thought, let's give it a go. I have done three unpaid talks just to get a feel for it, and from it, I have set myself yet another challenge: before I DIE, I will be on TED Talks. Imagine that FOOL of the School on TED Talks, sharing his experience and knowledge.

Yes, Mr Douglas, my R.E. teacher, if you're reading this, I will do it to prove you wrong. 😊

11 - Income from rental properties.

I had a rental property for ten years but recently sold it. In hindsight, I should have kept it going, but I needed extra capital to raise additional funds for a deposit on a new house.
It gave a brilliant yearly yield of £3,600.00 net profit each year off one property, which helped towards a family holiday. Plus, the inflation of the property value each year.
I would strongly recommend doing some research into property investing and building a little portfolio of your own to pay for the luxuries and lifestyle you wish for.

12 – YouTube.

I have started up a YouTube channel, BB410YOWHY; on it will be these books in digital video format with the goal that when I receive over a million views in the next ten years there will be an income generated from it.

13 – Gold investment for the long term.

Gold has kept its value over centuries, making it a reliable store of wealth even in the face of economic downturns or other issues. That's why many investors turn to the precious metal during uncertain times; it can reliably protect their wealth.

At 16 years old, in 10 years, you'll be 26 with a wealth of knowledge. Small monthly investments lead to big results. The key is taking the one step on the yellow road to wealth.

Part 1 - INVESTMENTS

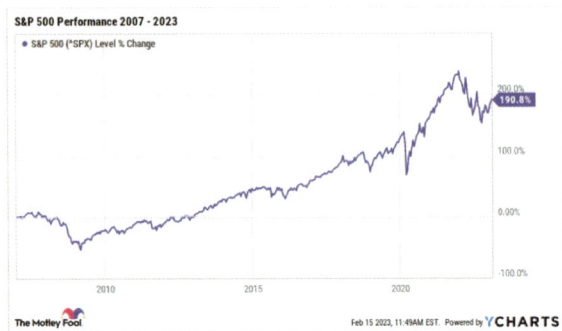

S&P 500 Performance 2007 - 2023
● S&P 500 (^SPX) Level % Change

The Motley Fool — Feb 15 2023, 11:49AM EST. Powered by YCHARTS

Above is a graph showing 500 businesses in America and how they are performing.

If you've read the Business Book For 10-Year-Olds...WHY? you will know I touched on investments.

On average, investments have a yearly yield of 10% compounded over a 10-year span. This would have given a nice, healthy return if the economic climate had been right at the time. For instance, there was a financial crash in 2008, and people and businesses lost millions; more recently, a pandemic, many businesses closed and crashed.

If you were 67 at the retirement age plus had investments to draw down on, there is a possibility that a lot of your money would be in a negative loss due to the stock market crash.

It's all about timing; some have more luck than others. I do think the harder people work the luckier they will be, but when it comes to stock market crashes, there is absolutely nothing anyone can do. Sometimes, the big crashes happen overnight.

But the smart business owners amongst the population take advantage of this situation and BUY the stocks and shares when they are low, in anticipation that they will get a better "ROI" Return on Investment.

You may have heard the quote or saying, "Don't put all your eggs in one basket," this happens with investments, too.

You will need to speak to a financial advisor to get professional advice, but my take would be to do some research into Personal Pension Investment, Property Investing, ETF exchange trading funds, minerals and metals investments, crypto, plus many others.

These will all give you an average of 8% - 10% ROI per annum on your investment. As I've mentioned previously money going to work for you, not the other way round.

I invest with a company called Fundsmith, which was set up by a chap called Terry Smith; they invest in equities on a global basis.

The company's approach is to be a long-term investor in its chosen stocks.

It will not adopt short-term trading strategies.

The company has stringent investment criteria, which Fundsmith LLP and Fundsmith Investment Services Limited, as investment managers, adhere to in selecting securities for the company's investment portfolio.

These criteria aim to ensure that the company invests in:

- High-quality businesses that can sustain a high return on operating capital employed.
- Businesses whose advantages are difficult to replicate.
- Businesses which do not require significant leverage to generate returns.
- Businesses with a high degree of certainty of growth from reinvestment of their cash flows at high rates of return.
- Businesses that are resilient to change, particularly technological innovation.
- Businesses whose valuation is considered by the Company to be attractive.

The company will not invest in derivatives and will not hedge any currency exposure arising from within the operations of an investee business nor from the holding of an investment denominated in a currency other than sterling.

Please note that with any investment, there are **Principal Risks,** such as:

- The value of companies invested in, and therefore the value of the fund, will rise and fall, and there is no guarantee that you will get your investment back.
- An investment in the fund should only be made by those persons who are able to sustain a loss on their investment.
- The Shares should be viewed as long-term investments (at least five years).
- The fund's portfolio is a global portfolio, and many of the investments are not denominated in GBP.
- There is no currency hedging made by the fund.
- The GBP price of the shares may, therefore, rise or fall purely on account of exchange rate movements.

Having said that, the application of the investment criteria described above significantly limits the number of potential investments: the fund generally invests in 20 to 30 stocks, and so it is more concentrated than many other funds. This means that the performance or underperformance of a single stock has a greater effect on the price of the fund.

If you are unsure about the suitability of the fund for you, please seek professional advice.

At the time of writing this book, Fundsmith Portfolio Comment for April 2023:

- They began a current small holding in Procter & Gamble.
- The top 5 contributors in the month were Meta Platforms, Microsoft, L'Oréal, Novo Nordisk, and McCormick.
- The top 5 detractors were IDEXX, Automatic Data Processing, Waters, Mettler-Toledo, and Estée Lauder.

Top 10 holdings (at the time of writing this 05.05.23. 00:23hrs)

1. Microsoft
2. Novo Nordisk
3. L'Oréal
4. LVMH
5. Philip Morris
6. Stryker
7. IDEXX
8. Meta Platforms
9. McCormick
10. Estee Lauder

Fundsmith knows just a small number of high-quality, resilient, global growth companies that are good value, and which they intend to hold for a long time, and in which they invest their own money.

Part 2 - Crypto – Cryptocurrency & What is it?

As previously mentioned, I have also invested in crypto since 2017, and what a journey that's been.

At the age of 16, most of you will be aware of crypto, which you have seen on all your social media platforms.

For those who do not know, cryptocurrency is a digital currency, which is an alternative form of payment created using encryption algorithms.

The use of encryption technologies means that cryptocurrencies function both as a currency and as a virtual accounting system.

My portfolio consists of Bitcoin, Ethereum, & Lite Coin.

Is cryptocurrency a good investment?

The truth is that cryptocurrency is an extremely volatile asset.

You need to understand that owning crypto involves taking on a great deal of risk in their portfolios.
But for investors who understand how to manage risk, crypto could present great opportunities.

How does crypto turn into money?

You can use a crypto exchange like Coinbase, Kucoin, or Kraken to turn Bitcoin into cash. This may be an easy method if you already use a centralised exchange and your crypto lives in a custodial wallet. Choose the coin and amount you would like to sell, agree to the rates, and your cash will be available to you.

For me, I have little knowledge of crypto because it was new at the time. There has been a huge crash in the year 2021 to 2022, with people and businesses losing enormous amounts of their investments. Recently, we have seen exponential growth and massive gains. This has been the pattern over many years.

There is an application (app) called "Coinbase" that gives you all the real-time data on how the stocks are performing.

Like most investments, this is a risk; some people and businesses make a ton of money, and some do not. It's like a form of gambling because you never know the true outcome.

As I author this book, I am NOT a professional financial advisor, and I do not have any qualifications; in fact, the only qualification I have is a diploma in business management.

I am simply just giving you an insight into my portfolio of investments; you must seek professional advice; these advisors are called IFAs Independent Financial Advisors before committing to anything to do with money.

However, I will tell you a little secret: I did not and have not paid for an IFA; I am just a bit of a RISK taker.

I say all the time, as I previously mentioned in the other chapter, it is better to live a life and say, "I am glad I gave that a go," rather than, "I wish I did that."

Part 3 - PENSIONS

You may or may not have heard of a pension; if you have, you will think,

"Only old people have pensions."

I promise you when you are 45 years old, you will say, "I am so glad I read Business Book For 16-Year-Olds...WHY? and started planning for my retirement."

A pension is a tax-efficient way of saving money for your retirement.

There are different types of pensions. One of the most common is a workplace pension, where both you and your employer save (or contribute) into a pension. You may also have a personal or private pension that you've set up for yourself. You can save into several different pensions if you stay within your annual and lifetime limits.

To encourage you to save into your pension, the government also adds money to them through pension tax relief. The amount of tax relief will depend on your circumstances, and, of course, tax rules may change in the future.

Remember, as with any investment, the value of your pension and any income may fall and rise and is not guaranteed.

When you reach age 55 (rising to 57 in 2028), you can take the money from your pension as an income, a lump sum, or a combination of both.

How does the pension work?

With a defined contribution pension scheme, you pay a percentage of your salary, and your employer also contributes to it. The pension provider then invests the contributions. The income you get in retirement is not guaranteed – it depends on how much has been contributed and the performance of the investments.

What is the simple definition of pension?

Pension. Noun. Pen·sion.: money paid under given conditions to a person following retirement or to surviving dependents; see also defined benefit plan, defined contribution plan.

You are reading Business Book For 16-Year-Olds..WHY? so it's highly likely you're going to be a super successful business owner, so the laws are different with pensions as they would be as an employee.

What are the best types of pensions for Business Owners/self-employed people?

Personal/Private pension.

Self-Invested Personal Pension (SIPP)

National Employment Savings Trust (Nest)

Lifetime ISA (LISA)

How much can my Ltd company pay into my pension?

Currently, there is no limit to how much you are allowed to pay into a pension. However, there is a limit to how much you can invest and still claim tax relief.

This is currently set at 100% of your earned income, up to £60,000 a year – the Annual Allowance (A.A.).

If you are self-employed, you are entitled to the State Pension in the same way as anyone else.

When you set up a business, you become self-employed, which means you work for yourself. More on being self-employed in the next chapter, but for now, we are talking about pensions.

There are many ways to become a business owner; you can be a registered CIC charity business or partnership plus others, which again we will talk about in the next chapters, but one of them is a Private Limited Company (PLC). As previously mentioned, one of my businesses is a Private Limited Company called MDFITOUT LTD; we refurbish commercial office space, retail units, shops, and industrial units.

So, how do pensions work for limited companies?

Your limited company can contribute pre-taxed company income to your pension. Because an employer contribution counts as an allowable company pension scheme business expense, your company receives tax relief against corporation tax, so the company could save up to 25% in corporation tax.

I have a private pension scheme, which is paid for through my company and which I pay monthly. As previously mentioned, this is a TERRIFIC way to reduce your corporation tax bill.

More about HMRC tax liabilities in the next book, Business Book For 18-Year-Olds.WHY?

To summarise the investments, as you can see, my portfolio does not have all its eggs in one basket.

1. Private Investments
2. Crypto Currencies
3. Private Pensions
4. Government State Pensions

For some of you, most of this information will not have been spoken about in your homes because money causes anxiety and stress.

It is a curse handed down from generation to generation.

Chapter 4 – WHY NOW?

SO WHY NOW...? You are only sixteen. Surely you do not need to start now.

Continue reading to find the benefits of starting now.

1. Sense of security: Investing and saving money can supply a sense of security and stability. It can help reduce the stress that comes with financial insecurity.

2. Financial Independence: If you start saving and investing at a young age, you are more than likely to become financially independent later in life. This independence will give you a profound sense of control over your life.

3. Confidence: Building a financial foundation can instill confidence in your life to make better decisions as you get older. You will build a wealth so great that your children and grandchildren will benefit from it. How amazing would it be knowing you are going to leave a legacy for your own family?

4. Unforeseen Circumstances: Life is unpredictable, and having savings in place ensures that you are prepared for unforeseen circumstances, such as job loss or unexpected medical expenses if you live in the USA or in a country other than the United Kingdom. For international readers, the United Kingdom has an NHS, which stands for National Health Service, where all medical treatment is free. Some people do pay for their own private health care, but for the majority, healthcare is provided for.

5. Freedom: Freedom to take risks; investing from an early age will allow you to take calculated risks with your savings, which can lead to longer-term gains.

There are some great positives of investing and saving at an early age; this is great when life is flowing, you have good people around you, and you are happy and content in yourself. HOWEVER, sometimes life likes to throw curve balls and set us off track a little.

Read on to find out some of the NEGATIVES about saving and investing from the early age of sixteen.

We hear daily, more so now than ever, about mental health and its effects on people. Anxiety and panic attacks have been at an all-time high; this can happen to you if you focus too much on your finances and neglect other aspects of your life.

Your social life will be nonexistent because you will be saving and investing whilst most of your friends are out spending on high street fashion clothes, eating out at restaurants, especially fast-food restaurants because they are convenient to go to and "chill out" whilst having some "grub" (that's an army saying for food).

You could be so fixated on saving your money that you become unwilling to take the risks and become focused on preserving your hard-earned cash. Saving money is great for rainy days but not making money, which is what Business Book For 16-Year-Olds...WHY? is all about, isn't it?

You have bought this book to learn innovative ideas so you can live the life you see on social media platforms, nice bags, expensive cars, and houses.

As you become older, in your mid-forties, you will realise that having those things is not what makes you the happiest. What makes you the happiest is living a life of purpose.

It is great to have a lot of money because you can help so many others less fortunate than you.

One of the biggest negatives of investing and saving at a young age is if a global pandemic hits again, with all your investments tied up, you could end up losing so much. At the time of writing this book, billions of pounds were lost in the stock markets and crypto practically overnight.

Unfortunately, that is the nature of the beast; some investments are super profitable, and some are not.

Imagine being at an early age and losing all your money; this will more than likely lead to frustration and loss of trust in the investment process, which in turn will have a detrimental effect on your portfolio.

On the other side, the best investors say "BUY, BUY, BUY" when the stocks are low; after a financial crash, historically, they understand, "what goes down must go up," data for the last 40 years and more has proven.

It is a big cycle that can be very profitable if good fortune is on your side.

CHAPTER 5 – Good Fortune, The Law of Attraction, & What's This Got to Do with Business?

I accept & allow
success
in all areas
of my life.

Good Fortune

The Law of Attraction is the belief that our thoughts, emotions and actions can attract positive or negative experiences into our lives.

This means that if we focus on positive thoughts and emotions, we will attract positive experiences, while if we focus on negative thoughts and emotions, we will attract negative experiences.

Good Karma, on the other hand, refers to the principle of cause and effect, where our actions and intentions have consequences that can influence our future experiences.

This means that if we do good things and have good intentions, we can expect good things to happen to us in the future.

The Law of Attraction

The Law of Attraction and good karma emphasise the importance of positive thinking and actions in creating a positive future.

By focusing on positive thoughts and actions, we can create a better future for ourselves and those around us.

As the legendary Uncle Ben Parker from the Marvel comics said once to Peter Parker (aka Spiderman):

"With Great Power Comes Great Responsibility".

What's This Got to Do with Business?

To relate this to the Business Book For 16-Year-Olds...WHY?

You will become wealthier than most of your friends or certainly wealthier than the 16-year-olds who have been domestically educated by the schooling systems to just get up, go to work, day in and day out, five or six days a week and go on one holiday a year.

Live a standard life, which, I might add, is PERFECTLY fine; we all live wonderfully weird lives, but being wealthy, you will have more responsibility.

You will more than likely have a team around you that you will need to support financially; no enormous success has ever been achieved by a single person.

You build your team, and together, you build your success with everyone rewarded one way or another.

This comes back to good karma; if you go about with bad intentions and "screw" people over in the process, trust me, it will come back and bite you on the bum.

You must have good intentions in everything you do; you will get magnificent pleasure from being wealthy if you have a good purpose.

A good purpose is giving to charities; volunteering your time more than your money will have an incredible impact on your life for the better.

In the next chapter we will talk about putting everything together and how to make a start.

Chapter 6 – READY, STEADY, ACTION...!

The last word is ACTION...!!! The time is nigh!

We read/watch so much on social media platforms about how we can get rich or how we can live a better life; we hear other people talking about what they are doing to better themselves.

HOWEVER, people never seem to take actual action.

We sit for so long and make ourselves believe we are taking action but never actually do the things that will improve our lives.

In this chapter, Business Book For 16-Year-Olds...WHY? we will plan a formula in which we can write down and START DOING.

The longer you leave it, the less you won't do it. I've waited 42 years to start doing it. My dad, who I love to bits, taught me hard work, he taught me integrity, he taught me the traditional way to go to work, "Get a job, son, and work hard".

Yes, this is true. You do have to work hard, but you can have money and work hard too.

Refer back to Chapter 3, Multiple Streams of Income and Investments; this is where money makes money without you having to do any physical labour.

In the boxes below, write down what's most important to you at this moment, not in a few years' time, as we will cover that in Business Book For 18-Year-Olds…WHY?

Saving?
Working for someone else?
Owning a business?
Investing?

1.	3.
2.	4.

Now, let's think about your answers!

Having a job at your age, 16, should be number one. This will give you money straight away, the main source of income, then investing, then saving, then owning a business.

Here are the reasons why, remember this is only my opinion. I am the FOOL OF THE SCHOOL, remember, but here goes.

1. Job = Your Time = payment

2. Payment = Investment = more payment (in the long term)

3. Savings = Just in case anything happens you haven't planned for

4. Owing a business = Freedom to choose what you want to do = Good Life.

Remember, you're just 16 and have the rest of your life ahead of you.

Working on number four takes patience, creativity, and perseverance, so it's a good option to have an income coming into your bank each month while you're finding your path for the first year or two. Sometimes, we never find our path we just keep on searching.

"I am a firm believer in throwing away the
map and get wonderfully lost".

Chapter 7 – Let's make MONEYYYY!!!!

In business we should try our best to have an end goal in mind and head for it. Always start at the end and work your way back.

Idea	How	Goal
Candle wax melts.	Sell ten candles per month at £8 per candle.	£80 each month
Walk people's dogs.	Find four different dog owners and walk their dogs at £10 per dog each day for five days a week for one hour.	£800 each month
Car valeting.	Clean the inside of cars, not the outside, for £10 per car. Take one hour on it. Twelve cars per month = three cars a week.	£120 each month

Now we have our total goal, £1000 per month, look at the hours worked.

Days	Hours	Weeks

As you can see, there are not that many hours worked for £1000.00 per month; with this in mind, you can set up other side hustles to create "multiple streams of income".

The goal is to have various types of income flowing into your bank so you can live a life you've always dreamed of and not depend on anyone else.

Write in the boxes your END GOAL, what you would like to achieve, and how you are going to get there.

IDEA	HOW	GOAL

After achieving your goals in the next ten years, you'll be 26 years old; believe it or not, some of you reading this book will have CHILDREN of your own.

If you start TODAY, you will have built up a business for the last ten years, which will be super successful by then; remember that you will FAIL.

"When it comes to achieving your goals, your failures are nothing more than success in progress".

"You are the future; you must provide a platform so your children can have the best possible start in their lives".

As the late John Haynes would say,
"FLY HIGH, MY LITTLE EAGLES."

Epilogue/Conclusion

If you have gotten this far, you will be successful; you have determination and ambition, you have drive, and you want a better life for yourself and others.

WELL, DONE! I am super proud of you. No matter what happens in your life, from this moment on, you have ACCOMPLISHED reading a book that no one has told you to read.

You have done it for yourself.

YOU ARE ONLY 16!

Tag me with #iread Business Book For 16- year-olds...WHY?

You will be able to connect with other 16-year-olds who have also read this book.
You can talk on Facetime to anyone around the world and share each other's ideas.
Who knows, you might even set up a business with someone from this circle of trust.

In the next book, Business Book For 18-Year-Olds...WHY? we will cover tax in more detail in relation to allowable expenses and what you are legally allowed to claim when you do your Self-Assessment tax returns.

You can claim FLIGHTS abroad if you show that at some point you did some self-promoting or marketing of your business; you can claim 50% of the meals you eat and the hotel/accommodation you stay in.

This is the difference between a person who can afford to go on one or maybe two holidays a year and someone who goes on four or five like I did when I visited six countries in the year 2022, where I was able to claim most of the "business" trips in various countries other than the United Kingdom which is my country of residence.

Bibliography

What is a bibliography?

A bibliography is the list of sources a work's author used to create the work.

For instance, I went onto Google and typed in "What is a bibliography?" as I have used someone else's research, it is ethical and courteous to give recognition.

Throughout this book, there have been various references and photos. Please see the list below.

Pg 1 - "A foreword is a piece of writing, sometimes placed at the beginning of a book or other piece of literature." extract from www.wikipedia.co.uk.

Pg 2 - Various comments from extracted from www.Amazon.co.uk

Pg 4 - Self-comparison image by Chibird

Pg 4 - The school systems have been saying since you started school that if you are an A-grade student, you will be successful; if you do not have any grades, you will not. Podcast episode unknown by Mr Steven Bartlett www.stevenbartlett.com

Pg 5 – Photo/image online photos source unknown.

Pg 7 – Did you know that data from the Gallup World Poll (a survey of the happiness of adults in 132 countries around the WORLD) show that richer people in any country do not always feel happier than poorer ones? And beyond $75,000 a year in the United States, more money does not buy any more happiness at all for the average U.S. citizen earning about this amount. Research from the book Happiness By Design authored by Paul Dolan and published by Bolinda Publishing Pty Ltd.

Pg 8 - Photo/image online photos source unknown.

Pg 8 - *The Journey of 1000 Miles Starts with a Single Step.* March 20, 2017, | 6years | Press Releases. Giglets Education, as it is today, was founded in 2011 giglets.

YOUR NOTES

What Have You Learned That You Can Teach
Others

In this section, if you have been inspired and would like to set up a business, what would that be and why? Be as creative as possible.

This section is for you to write anything you want so that you can keep referring to it.

YOUR VISION

The following pages are blank – be as creative as possible…!

YOUR PLAN

YOUR NOTES

YOUR NOTES

YOUR NOTES

YOUR NOTES

YOUR NOTES

YOUR NOTES

YOUR NOTES

YOUR NOTES

YOUR NOTES

By Buying This Book, You Are Helping Two Charities.

CHARITY NO 1 – Incubabies Charity Number 1174162

The purpose of the charity is to raise funds for new equipment for the Neo-Natal Intensive Care Unit at Arrow Park Hospital, Wirral. Babies are born and need 24-hour care to give them the best possible start to life.

They do this through a series of fundraising activities run on an entirely voluntary basis.

They have no paid employees.

CHARITY NO 2 – Claire House Children's Hospice
Charity Number 1004058

Claire House Children's Hospice helps seriously and terminally ill children live life to the full by creating wonderful experiences and bringing back a sense of normality to family life.

By supplying specialist nursing and end-of-life care, as well as emotional support, Claire House helps families through some of the toughest times of their lives.

Now you have read the book, please think about the babies you have helped at the start of their journey, and when you close the book, think of the children you have helped who are at the end of their journey.

WE SUPPORT

IncuBabies
Big ambitions for tiny lives

Claire House
CHILDREN'S HOSPICE

A final note to all children:

"Never Give Up on Your Dreams."

Printed in Great Britain
by Amazon

54737067R00046